Dumfrie...

Through the Lens

Glimpses of old

Whithorn

Dumfries and Galloway Libraries,
Information and Archives
with Whithorn Photographic Group
1997

First published 1997
© Text copyright Whithorn Photographic Group
© Publication copyright Dumfries and Galloway Council

Designed by Dumfries and Galloway Libraries, Information and Archives. Set and printed by Solway Offset Services, Catherinefield Industrial Estate, Dumfries for the publisher.

Dumfries and Galloway Libraries, Information and Archives
Central Support Unit, Catherine Street
Dumfries DG1 1JB

ISBN 0 946280 23 1
Whithorn is number 2 in the
Dumfries and Galloway : *Through the Lens* series.
For a full list of our publications write to the above address.

ACKNOWLEDGEMENTS

This publication was funded by Groundbase Ltd., the Calouste Gulbenkian Foundation and Dumfries and Galloway Libraries, Information and Archives whose support for this project is greatly appreciated.

Our thanks also to Hilary More of the Department for Community Resources, Dumfries and Galloway Council for her support and help in organising this project.

The following, among others, have generously donated photographs for reproduction; without their help, this volume could not have been published:

John Adair, Jim Allan, Mrs Baxter, Mr D Bell, Ethel Brolls, Dr G Brown, Judy Brown, Rosemary Cameron, Mr and Mrs Chamberlain, Margaret Cronie, Margaret Donaldson, Mrs E Drape, Morag Fisher, Lis Graham, the Herald and Evening Times, Mr and Mrs Jaques, Ruby Kirk, William Lawrie, Mr D Lester, Clifford Longridge, Fiona McLellan, Jock McMaster, Mary McShane, John McWilliam, Mrs M Martin, Mr James Maxwell, Sir Michael Maxwell, Mrs C Millar, John Mills, George Moore, Mrs E J Murray, Miss J Murray, Mr C Sandbach, John Scoular, Mr and Mrs Stewart, Sandra Templeton, Isobel Torbet, Joe Whiteford and the Whithorn Trust.

The plate on page 22 is Crown Copyright: Reproduced by courtesy of Historic Scotland.

PROFITS FROM THE SALE OF THIS BOOK GO TO SUPPORT THE SOUTH MACHARS COMMUNITY CENTRE.

INTRODUCTION

There is an inevitable nostalgia in glimpsing the past through old photographs. The camera gives us a deceptively intimate acquaintance with its subjects, which is tempered by our awareness that the faces captured by it are often now long gone and sometimes nameless. An entire way of life and, often, the very buildings which housed it, and the technologies which made it possible, can have vanished. Therein lie the fascination, the charm, the poignancy and also the historic value of old photographs.

In these views of the Royal Burgh of Whithorn, taken largely between 1890 and 1950, we have attempted to show a small sample of an unsuspectedly large volume of material. We have chosen a cross-section of pictures, to demonstrate the variety and the vibrancy of life in the town during this period, when it was buoyed up by a labour-intensive agricultural economy and not yet noticeably affected by an increasing centralisation and concentration of all kinds of services in larger centres.

Some of these photographs have come from postcards, either by local or national professional photographers, others come from professional photographs intended for private use; still others are private snapshots. All came from private collections in the Southern Machars and this very fact has enriched our knowledge of the pictures, since, with them, there were often preserved precious fragments of information, names and dates, which have brought the prints to life.

We hope that others will share our pleasure in the discovery of each print and each new view. We also hope that the enjoyment given by this collection will persuade others to preserve photographs, negatives, slides and the information and folklore which are often handed down with them.

WHITHORN PHOTOGRAPHIC GROUP,
July 1997

J DRAPE AND SONS' IRONMONGERY WAREHOUSE

This photograph of the family business of J Drape and Sons, saddlers and ironmongers, was taken by Kay's Photographic Studios, Stranraer, at some point prior to 1884. Drape's was a Whithorn institution for 160 years; it was already registered as a saddler's in Pigot's Commercial Directory of Whithorn tradesmen of 1837. Later, both Drape's and D Niven's businesses moved premises to new purpose-built shops in St John Street. The building on the right, which appears to be the store, was burnt down and rebuilt in 1934.

McKNAUGHT'S SHOP, THE PEND
Whithorn appears to have been well-provided with ironmongery shops, since McKnaught's shop, taken at roughly the same period in the 1880's, appears to be selling oil-lamps and bellows; one of the boys among the interested onlookers is seated on a copper, used for boiling clothes.

THE PEND AND TRADERS

Another photograph from Kay's Studios, which seems to have been taken very shortly after that of Drape's warehouse, on the same day, judging by the cart (on the extreme left of the picture) which has not yet driven off. The two houses on the right in the foreground were later demolished and replaced by Muir's emporium; the gaps in numbering of houses at this point in George Street bear testimony to the earlier layout. A small girl operates the water pump in the right foreground.

2 GEORGE STREET WITH GIGS
There is an impressive collection of gigs in this picture of the most northerly part of George Street, taken once again by Kay's, Stranraer. One assumes that there was a special reason for the assemblage of men and children - perhaps a meeting in the public rooms at the adjacent Grapes Hotel.

2 GEORGE STREET
 J S THOMSON, IRONMONGER: This close-up of the same building, at roughly the same date, shows a sample of the wares on sale at another Whithorn ironmongery: washing coppers, barrels, portmanteaux and oil-lamps.

A K MUIR'S SHOP, 45-7 GEORGE STREET
We are fortunate in having all the names of the shop staff in this picture of A K Muir's Grocery: from left to right, they are Stewart Heron, Jeanie Stewart, James Muir, A K Muir, James Anderson, George Hannah and Thomas Whannell. The horse's name was Liza and she pulls a spring-cart, used for deliveries. The business was founded in 1870, according to an inscribed sandstone pediment which used to stand above the centre of the building, but the building itself dates from 1901 and replaces the buildings shown in plate 3. Later it became a plumbing business, a grocer's, delicatessen and general store; it now houses the Whithorn Excavation Visitor Centre.

7

THE PEND, WITH PROVOST MCKEAND

The Pend, with its fifteenth century arch, with arms of Bishop Vaux, and Royal coat of arms of Scotland, is still a focus of the burgh and a reminder of Whithorn's ecclesiastical greatness. Here it is shown around 1900 in a photograph by Whithorn photographer, J N Alves, who ran a jeweller's and watchmaker's business at 2 George Street. He published a great number of postcard views of the town and surrounding area, and an *Album of Views of Whithorn and the Isle of Whithorn.*

CASTLEHILL CORNER

This street-scene of Whithorn children, taken between 1900 and 1905, was carefully conserved by the family of the two children on the extreme right, who were visiting the town for the day. They were Alex and Agnes McCaig, Challoch Farm, Leswalt. The house on the left corner later became the home of Cathy Hughes, who was well known as a seller of fine confectionery; in this picture it supports street gas lighting, previously, it had been the Commerical Inn. The bank building on the extreme right now has lost its balustrading and finials above the front door.

GRAPES HOTEL, c.1930
This view of the town shows one of the bakers Willie Horner, who worked for Denton's bakery, a well-known Whithorn institution, housed at 2 and 4 George Street. In the background is the Grapes Hotel, a focus for the burgh for 190 years, with its prominent roof-top sign.

G B DRAPE AND APPRENTICES, 65 ST JOHN STREET
By 1884, Drape's ironmongery had moved to 65 St John Street, where it was run by three successive generations of the Drape family. In the centre stands G B Drape, with the Bendal brothers on either side; the small boy apprentice is Johnny Flannighan. From the sign, it appears that the shop dealt in roofing felt, as well as the ubiquitous oil-lamps.

11

DRAPE'S SHOP, 1935
The shop windows are here decked out for the King George V's and Queen Mary's Silver Jubilee in 1935, with further posters explaining the benefits of electricity. This was installed in Whithorn in 1936. The boy on the left is Billy Hawthorn, who was employed in the shop from the end of the Second World War until 1984; the girls are Sarah and Elizabeth Drape.

THE WINDMILL STUMP

An operating windmill at the top of the town in Whithorn was marked on Ainslie's map of 1785, where houses at Kilncroft now are. By the time this picture was taken, the *Windmill Stump* and had been converted into an unusual sort of tenement. One resident we know of was a Mr McGhie, but a lengthy rhyming verse refers to a Tarrie Glancer, who sold old clothes, and to whom the narrator protests

> *But, Mr Glancer, this fine hoose*
> *Of yours is not in fashion*
> *I do not think the like is found*
> *In any other nation.*

The remains of the Stump were eventually bulldozed in the 1960's.

MISS BIE'S SHOP
This view shows the top of the town prior to re-development by the Town Council. On the extreme right there is a glimpse of the last thatched house in Whithorn, occupied by the Maxwell family. Miss Bie and her sister sold groceries.

MCKELVIE'S SHOP, GLASSERTON STREET
Standing either side of the front door are the McKelvie brother and sister, who ran a licensed grocer's from the premises.

ST JOHN STREET UNITED FREE CHURCH

This church was built in 1892 by the architect's firm of Thomson and Sandilands and appears in this photograph with elegant railings, rooflights and trees surrounding it. The 1892 building replaced a Secession church which had been on the site since the 1760's and it may be that the name of St John Street harks even further back, to land owned by the Knights of St John, who provided hospitality to pilgrims on their way to shrines. At one point, Whithorn had five churches, including a Cameronian Meeting House in what is now Drill Hall Lane. After the reunification of the United Free Church with the Church of Scotland in 1937, the church building was no longer needed and became a feed store and, now, a garage. Note the water pump in the foreground.

ST JOHN STREET, WITH SPIRE
Taken facing northwards and showing the spire of St John Street's United Free Church, now a garage, this picture shows a corner of the New Town Hall built 1884 and an array of advertising signs on the notice board for furniture and carpets.

THE MEET 1902
This dramatic picture of the Glasserton Hunt coming through the town centre shows one of the occasions on which the people of the burgh would have encountered the inhabitants of the great houses in the surrounding countryside. The Glasserton estate was also an important employer, requiring large numbers of both men and women to staff the house, grounds, kitchen garden, stables and home farm.

18

STREET BAND, GEORGE STREET

Probably roughly contemporary with the other view (page 9) from Castlehill corner, this photograph shows a marching band and its crowd of onlookers. On the right is the Brunswick Inn, one of three hostelries, of which the local rhyme, parodying a popular advertisement for fountain-pens, went

They come as a boon and a blessing to men
The Brunswick, the Grapes and the yin at the Pen'.

STILT-WALKER, GEORGE STREET

Another form of popular entertainment is shown in this remarkable picture of a tall stilt act, watched attentively by the little girl in the foreground. Perhaps this was a prelude to a full circus visit to the town; Pinder's circus is known to have visited. A child of parents with a circus act, who was taken ill while passing through Whithorn, is buried in the churchyard.

THE BIG SNOW 1947

The Railway Inn, St John Street, appears in this picture as virtually buried under a huge fall of snow, which took place in 1947. Others similarly dramatic occurred at the turn of the century and in 1940, when Whithorn and surrounding farms and villages were cut off for 2 to 3 weeks from supplies; food was dropped at the Isle by aircraft.

EXCAVATION TEAM, WHITHORN PRIORY, 1890's
The Third Marquess of Bute [1847-1900], a devout Roman Catholic, as well as an antiquarian and architectural connoisseur of distinction, made a sustained attempt during the 1890's, to find evidence for Whithorn's mediaeval and early Christian past and to restore parts of the Priory, which had lain more or less buried for centuries. Thanks to his inspiration and the industry of his excavation team, led by the architect William Galloway, the extraordinary collection of Christian stones, including the earliest Christian monument in Scotland, were rescued and put on display in Whithorn museum. During this period, Cruggleton Church, St Ninian's Chapel, Isle of Whithorn, and the Old Place of Mochrum were also similarly restored.

ST NINIAN'S COMMEMORATION SERVICE, 16 SEPTEMBER 1932

This impressive parade of clergymen, which occurred on St Ninian's Day 1932, marked the 1500th anniversary of the date when, traditionally, Scotland's first Christian bishop and Whithorn's founder, St Ninian, was held to have died on 16 September, 432 AD. The procession and praise were led by the Moderator of the Church of Scotland and the Episcopal Bishop of Glasgow and Galloway. 65 years later, in 1997, commemorative processions and celebrations were held to mark the sixth centenary of the traditional date of the founding by St Ninian of the church at Whithorn in 397 AD.

THE BIG SNOW 1947
This photograph of Whithorn under heavy snow shows the buildings on the right which were eventually demolished and the area reused as a site for the first Roman Catholic Church to have been built within the burgh boundary since the Reformation.

FOUNDATION STONE, ST MARTIN'S AND ST NINIAN'S CHURCH, 1959
The new Roman Catholic Church was dedicated in 1959, the new church replacing one which had been functioning until this date at High Mains Farm south of Whithorn. The Marquess of Bute had bought the farm, which stood on the burgh's boundaries, from the Earl of Galloway in the late nineteenth century, and, for a time, installed there a group of Premonstratensian canons, who had originally staffed Whithorn cathedral in the twelfth century. The new building in Whithorn opened as Parish Church on St. Ninian's Day 1960.

PILGRIMAGE TO ST NINIAN'S CAVE, 1936
The tradition of St Ninian's episcopate and evangelical work at Whithorn in the late fourth and early fifth centuries has always been kept alive in the Catholic Church and this photograph of a procession in 1936 shows the immense popularity of the traditional yearly pilgrimage on St Ninian's Day to the cave on Glasserton shore, where St Ninian is recorded to have retreated for meditation and solitude.

THE ROYAL VISIT JULY 1955
Shortly after her coronation, HM Queen Elizabeth II visited the burgh, the first monarch to renew the tradition of Royal visits to Whithorn in 400 years; her predecessors on the throne of Scotland came, sometimes annually, to pay homage at the shrine of St Ninian. The young woman at the front sitting with the school children is Dorothy Chamberlain.

THE QUEEN'S VISIT TO *CANDIDA CASA* 1955

Whithorn has seen a distinguished succession of archaeologists, seeking to discover the physical evidence which might bear out the tradition of a *shining white* early Christian church. In this photograph, the Queen is being shown the lime-plastered dwarf walls at the east end of the crypts, which were identified by C A Ralegh Radford [on her right] in the 1950's as the most likely candidate for St Ninian's church. On her left is Provost Arnott and R G Alexander, Town Clerk to the burgh.

WILLIE MCGINN
One of Whithorn's colourful personalities before the turn of the century, Willie McGinn sold fish and kept a large army of cats well fed at the tail of his cart. He is one of the few subjects who has posed cheerfully for the camera, but he appears, as an older man, in the picture of the pig-slaughter (inside front cover), looking considerably more grim.

WIFFY KEITH AND THE SCAVVY CART
Pictured here outside J H Baxter's Pharmacy is one of Whithorn's well-known characters, who operated a horse-drawn refuse collection service into the late 1950's. The dog was called Tiny.

MRS DRAPE'S FIRST CLASS, Junior II 1921
This class at Whithorn school was the first teaching assignment of Mrs G B Drape, who herself came from the Highlands. She recorded all the names of her pupils, some of whom still came to school barefoot in summer: from left to right P Huxtable, W Murray, McIntyre, W Garrick, J Hearton, A Hawkins, M Martin, J Douglas, G McGowan, G McMeeking, McCreadie, Alex Love; 2nd row: A Martin, M Broll, M Christine, J Henderson, Mary Agnew, I Dodds, Cath Murry, Bella Hannah, Grace Malone, Bunty McCallie; Front Row: J McGeoch, Garrick, J Boyce, Ambrose, Reid, S Keith, G Dickie, J Stewart, M Martin.

GEORGE DICKIE, ALIAS JACK BRENT
George Dickie appears in the Whithorn School photograph in the bottom row, third from the right. He had a remarkable career, joining the Scottish Army and subsequently deserting and finally joining the Communist Party and the Brigade which fought Fascism in the 1937 Spanish Civil War. He changed his name to Jack Brent and a biography of him was published in London in the 1950's. He returned to Whithorn on a regular basis to recruit for the Party.

WHITHORN RAILWAY STAFF 1922
Whithorn acquired a branch line of the Wigtownshire Railway in 1877, which closed to passenger traffic in the 1950's and finally closed to goods trains in 1964. The staff in this picture appear very formally dressed. From left to right, back row: Sam Allan, William Barrie, Cecil Arnott, Forsyth Dobie, John McLellan, Fowler Gordon and James Leopold. Front row, left to right, shows John McLellan Snr [Guard]; William *Massy* McMaster and John Hackett.

WHITHORN TRAIN, WIGTOWNSHIRE RAILWAY
The Station, now all but obliterated, was at the northernmost end of the burgh, but it was the southernmost station in Scotland. It was especially important in the shipment of fresh milk from the creameries to central markets. Later it became the means of transporting troops to and from the military camps along the coast during the Second World War. This photograph is early, probably from the 1880's.

DODD'S CART

Pictured here in Castlehill, the narrow vennel which runs up the side of the Grapes Hotel towards the stables and on to the Isle, is the cart and its owner, Mr Dodds, who ran a delivery and collection service to and from Whithorn station. The extensions to the Grapes Hotel immediately behind him have now been demolished.

BAND, OUTSIDE FREE KIRK, KING'S ROAD c.1914
Many of the skilled tradesmen and shopkeepers played an active role in the life of the community. The names of those in this band are from the front, right to left: William *Wow* Black [Town crier]; Henry Walker [Skeog House]; William Douglas [butcher]; John Martin jnr; John Martin Snr [shoemaker]; Charlie Costley [Grocer]; Jimmy Cain; W J Rennie; David Douglas [on ground] [butcher]; 2nd row: Robert Robertson; Wilson *Wiff* Martin; Alex Hanlin; John Henderson; William Hawthorn; Biddle Martin [shoemaker]; Johnny Henderson; Back: Joe Martin and Charles Coid [butcher].

BOYS' BRIGADE c.1914
Some of the same names appear among the staff of the Boys' Brigade; some were to be killed in the 1939-45 War. From back to front, left to right: Jock Nairn, Willie Martin, Robert Huxtable [killed]; Andrew Henderson, Jack Murray, Henry McLaughlan, Alex McMeekan, Willie Carson, Peter Robertson, Lt Robert Robertson, Wm J Rennie P/T [killed]; Dr Douglas, ? Campbell, Robert Heron, ? ?, Hector Keachie, Victor Christie, James Carson, James Bendal, Hugh McLauchlan, Rev D M Hendry, Lt Arthur Arnott, John Henderson, Alex Murphy, Robt Harkness, Kenneth Hawthorn, John Garrick, Cecil Arnott, Hugh McCutcheon, Jack Harrison, Joe Hale, Sgt Bertie Brown, Kenneth McLean, Capt Birchman, Alex Costley, Sgt James Nairn [killed]; Dixie Morrison, Staff Sgt John Henderson [lost a leg in the War], Staff Sgt L Morrison.

UNVEILING OF THE WAR MEMORIAL 1920

This dramatic picture shows the crowds mustered round the new war memorial to the Burgh's war-dead, unveiled by Sir Herbert Maxwell two years after the Great War. In both Whithorn and the Isle of Whithorn, there were still captured German cannon to remind local people of the grim reality of war at the Front. The firm of W Gibson, whose premises are shown in the background, were well-known local engineers. Sadly, it was to be less than two decades until more names were added to the memorial.